NORTH AND DURHAM
COUNTRY RECIPES

COMPILED BY
ANN GOMAR

RAVETTE BOOKS

Published by Ravette Books Limited
3 Glenside Estate, Star Road
Partridge Green, Horsham,
West Sussex RH13 8RA
(0403) 710392

Production: Oval Projects Ltd.
Cover design: Jim Wire
Typesetting: Repro-type
Printing & binding: Norhaven A/S

All recipes are given in Imperial and Metric
weights and measures. Where measurements
are given in 'cups', these are American cups,
holding 8 fluid ounces.

The recipes contained in this book are traditional
and many have been compiled from archival sources.
Every effort has been made to ensure that the recipes
are correct.

RECIPES

SOUPS and BEGINNINGS

FISH

POULTRY and GAME

PRESERVES, PICKLES and SAUCES

DRINKS

NORTHUMBERLAND AND DURHAM

The ancient Kingdom of Northumbria is today made up of four counties, Northumberland, County Durham, Tyne and Wear, and Cleveland with wide rivers, rolling hills, high mountains and a fine coastline, sheltered valleys and lonely moors. It has a turbulent and romantic past: raids by Viking invaders, the building of the Roman Emperor Hadrian's Wall, the effect of the Industrial Revolution, have all been influential on the people's character and diet. Trade with Europe has encouraged a variety of imported foods and there are strong links with Scandinavia, both in customs and cooking. Northumbrian people appreciate good food — both plain and wholesome, as well as dishes made from excellent local specialities.

Although an important industrial area, with grand cities, such as Newcastle upon Tyne, Durham and Cleveland, the region is one of the most prosperous farming areas in the country, producing high quality beef, barley and lamb. Blackface and the Cheviot sheep, which roam the Cheviot Hills, are two famous breeds.

Farms in the north are often grouped around square solid stone-built peel-towers, where the whole village would gather at times of attack from marauders — the cattle on the ground floor, women and children on the first floor and the men on the roof to defend the village.

Hadrian's Wall, originally 15 ft high, and topped by 6ft battlements, was begun in AD 120. The troops lived in forts, such as the one at Housesteads, where the remains of grain and barley storage buildings can be seen. Six or eight soldiers shared a pair of rooms, which had a verandah, under which they did their cooking. A typical Roman dinner party for wealthy people was known to include oysters, mussels and snails, boiled ham, roast venison, suckling pig, peacock and stuffed dormouse.

The region is well known for fresh local fish straight from the sea, lake or river, such as cod, haddock, whiting, plaice, shellfish of all sorts including lobsters, (which are usually sold boiled and ready to eat), salmon and trout. The local boats used for fishing the rich coastal waters of the North Sea are called cobles.

Cotherstone in Teesdale is famous as being the only village in Northumbria with a cheese of its own. It is made in a white or blue veined version from unpasteurised milk and is open-textured with a sharp flavour.

The region is rich in local traditions. One of them, which dates back to the days when the Vikings invaded the area, is held on New Year's Eve in Allendale, a lead mining town where the miners kept sheep on the fell. A huge bonfire is lit, the men parade round the lanes with blazing tar barrels on their heads, and 'first footing' takes place round the village with bread, coal, and silver.

At Tweedmouth a feast is held for one week in July, which starts with the crowning of the Salmon Queen, celebrating an industry in which the town has been involved for centuries.

Rhubarb and gooseberries are grown, both commercially and domestically. Gooseberry growing became so popular among the northern gardeners during the Industrial Revolution, that competitions to find the biggest gooseberry grower were held in the summertime. While the winter brought contests to find the leek-growing champion. The region's fondness for leeks has given rise to some popular specialities, in particular Leek Pudding and Leek Soup.

At Bedlington the Annual Miner's Gala and Picnic takes place with brass bands and beauty contests. The miners ate good substantial food, suet puddings, both sweet and savoury, and plenty of bread and potatoes; on Sundays, there was a huge meat dinner, often followed by rice pudding. Many miners were self-sufficient, growing vegetables and keeping chickens and rabbits, and often a pig, every bit of which was used at killing time. Prior to 1850, cooking in a collier's cottage would be done on an open fire, and baking in a communal oven with room for eight loaves, which the colliers' wives would take turns to stoke.

Cold Water Willies were hard flat biscuits made from flour and water when times were especially difficult. They were known as 'tough cake and pullit', because they had to be pulled apart to eat.

Every event was marked by ceremony and special food. Harvest was celebrated with kern suppers — at Allendale, the traditional fare was tattie pie. The end of the herring season was celebrated in villages along the coast, with feasts, which often featured bread and ham, entertainments, sideshows, and a tug-of-war.

The popularity of high tea in the home as well as tea parties for all sorts of occasions — chapel, church, Sunday school and the like, gave scope for local housewives' pride in home baking. Delicious cakes and teabreads still win prizes at local shows.

Strong, dark, full-bodied beer as brewed by the local breweries is a popular local beverage. Lindisfarne Mead is produced on the Holy Island of Lindisfarne, off the Northumbrian coast. The honey which is used for the mead is made from bees have been brought from all over the world. It is vatted with fermented grape juice and the pure natural water of an artesian well and fortified with fine sprits. The Romans and Vikings drank mead to give them greater virility; while newly weds were advised to drink mead for a whole moon (month) to increase their chances of a happy marriage. The word 'honeymoon' originates from this ancient custom.

The visitor to Northumbria will discover not only beautiful scenery, miles of deserted beaches, and a deep sense of history, but a wealth of good food.

'But we put the gordle on the rousing fire upon,
An' we whistled as we baked wor singin' hinney-o.
It's not fine claes nor drink,
Nor owt 'at ye can think,
Can had a cannle up ti singin' hinney-o.'

The Singin' Hinney, 1885

QUICK GOLDEN VEGETABLE SOUP

(Serves 4 as a lunch or supper dish, 6 as a starter)

In earlier centuries the main meal of the day for ordinary people was a hot bowl of steaming soup served with chunks of bread. This hearty soup uses light coloured vegetables — hence the name — and is delicious as a first course but substantial enough to serve as a lunch or supper dish of its own with crusty bread.

1 lb (450 g) potatoes
8 oz (225 g) onions
8 oz (225 g) carrots
8 oz (225 g) turnips
8 oz (225 g) celery
2 pints (1.15 litres/ 5 cups) chicken stock
Salt and pepper
Bouquet garni
1 oz (25 g) butter or margarine
1 oz (25 g) flour
Grated cheese or chopped chives to garnish

Peel the potatoes, onions, carrots, and turnips.

Finely chop the onions and celery.

Grate the potatoes, carrots, and turnips.

Put all the vegetables into a saucepan with the stock, and bouquet garni.

Season with salt and pepper.

Bring to the boil, and simmer for about 20 minutes until the vegetables are soft.

Blend the butter with the flour and stir into the soup.

Cook for five minutes longer.

Remove the bouquet garni.

Serve garnished with a little grated cheese or chopped chives.

LEEK AND POTATO SOUP

Serves 4-5

4 large leeks
A little butter for frying
1 lb (450 g) potatoes
2 pints (1.15 litres/ 5 cups) white stock
Salt and pepper
2½ fl oz (4 tablespoons/ ⅓ cup) cream

Trim, wash and cut the leeks into slices.

Peel and dice the potatoes.

Melt the butter in a saucepan and lightly fry the vegetables until soft but not coloured.

Pour on the stock, bring to the boil and simmer for about 20 minutes or until the vegetables are tender.

Sieve the soup or purée in an electric blender.

Return the mixture to the saucepan.

Heat again, season with salt and pepper to taste.

Swirl in the cream or add the milk just before serving.

LAKINS ELIZABETHIAN DELIGHT Serves 4

FROM LANGLEY CASTLE

Langley Castle Hotel at Langley-on-Tyne, near Hexham in Northumberland is close to Hadrian's Wall and its Roman forts. The castle has 7 feet thick walls, and the main staircase houses what are considered to be the finest remaining examples of 16th century garderobes in Europe.

8 oz (225 g) chopped cured ham
2 oz (50 g) butter
2 oz (50 g) demerara sugar
A pinch of cinnamon
Bought puff pastry vol-au-vent cases
Tomato and cucumber salad for garnish

Melt the butter, cinnamon and demerara sugar in a shallow frying pan.

Add the chopped cured ham and sauté until golden brown.

Pile the mixture into the vol-au-vent cases.

Serve with a light tomato and cucumber salad.

DURHAM BACON BROTH

Serves 4

¼ lb (100 g) spilt peas
8 bacon ribs
2 potatoes
2 carrots
½ turnip
1 parsnip
1 leek
¼ lb (100 g) barley

Cover the barley and spilt peas with boiling water to blanch, and leave to soak for 2 hours.

Put the bacon ribs in a large pan and cover them with water.

Bring to the boil and simmer for half an hour, then drain.

Peel and chop the potatoes, carrots, turnip and parsnip and chop the leek.

Add the vegetables to the bacon ribs.

Add the barley and spilt peas and simmer until cooked, adding more liquid if required.

Remove the bacon ribs before serving.

JUGGED KIPPERS FOR BREAKFAST

Serves 4

Craster in Northumberland is famous for delicious kippers, which are cured there in kippering sheds during the spring and summer months of the season. A kipper is a herring which has been split, salted and dried in smoke.

1 kipper per person
A knob of butter or margarine per person.

Wash the fish in cold water.

If required, cut off the head and trim with kitchen scissors.

Put the kipper, tail up, in a tall jug.

Pour on sufficient boiling water to cover the fish.

Leave to stand for 5-10 minutes or until tender.

Remove the fish from the jug and serve topped with a knob of butter.

KIPPERED EGGS

4 kippers
4 eggs
8 tablespoons milk
Pepper
4 oz (100 g) butter or margarine
1 round of toast per person
Butter or margarine for spreading

Cook the kippers in boiling water until tender.

Allow to cool.

Remove the skin and bones, and flake the flesh into small pieces.

Lightly beat the eggs together with the milk, and season the mixture with pepper.

Melt 4 oz (100 g) of butter or margarine in a saucepan.

Pour in the egg mixture, and add the fish.

Cook over a low heat, stirring continuously until the eggs set.

Serve on buttered toast.

KIPPER SAVOURY

These delicious toasts can also be served after dinner or if cut up into small squares, as a cocktail savoury.

2 kippers or 4 kipper fillets
4 fingers of toast
2 oz (50 g) grated cheese
A little parsley for garnish

Trim the kippers.

Put them into a basin or jug and pour on boiling water.

Leave to stand for 3 minutes, then drain.

Remove the skin and bone from the flesh.

Divide into 4 fillets and put each one on a finger of toast.

Sprinkle the savouries with grated cheese and brown under a hot grill.

Serve garnished with parsley.

SMOKED FISH CHOWDER

Serves 4

A favourite recipe of Elizabeth Steele, Curator of Raby Castle, Staindrop.
The delicious substantial chowder makes a meal in itself. North Shields
and Craster are renowned for very good smoked fish.

1 lb (450 g) smoked cod or haddock, skinned
1 lb (450 g) potatotes
4 oz (100 g) streaky bacon or pork belly
A little butter for frying if required
Milk and water to cover
A bay leaf
14 oz (400 g) cooked sweetcorn
1 medium onion, sliced
Pepper

Peel and chop the potatoes into bite sized pieces.

Roughly cube the haddock or cod.

Cut the bacon or pork into small cubes, and fry gently until
the fat runs — use a little butter if necessary.

Add the potatoes and onions, and let them sweat in the fat
produced.

Add the fish with the bay leaf, an cover with the milk and
water.

Let the mixture cook gently, making sure that it does not
stick, until the potatoes are very soft and the fish is cooked.

Flake the fish into the soup and add the corn.

Season with pepper to taste.

Continue cooking until the corn is very hot.

Serve in soup plates.

NORTHUMBERLAND TROUT IN CREAM

Serves 6

This recipe has been popular since the beginning of the century.

Allow about 8 oz (225 g) trout per person
¾ pint (450 ml/ 2 cups) thick double cream
Seasoned flour
2 glasses of white wine
1 cucumber
Salt
A knob of butter

Skin and clean the fish.

Brush them all over with some cream and sprinkle with the seasoned flour. Reserve the rest of the cream.

Put the fish in a greased casserole dish and cook in a moderate oven for 5 minutes on each side.

Add the wine and continue cooking for a further 10 minutes.

Pour on the remaining cream and cook for another 20 minutes.

Stir and season the sauce that is forming.

Dice the cucumber into ½ inch (1 cm) cubes.

Poach the cucumber gently in salted water with a knob of butter. Drain and keep hot.

When the fish is cooked, add the cucumber to the sauce in the casserole.

Return the dish to the oven for 2 minutes before serving straight from the casserole.

Oven: 350°F/180°C Gas Mark 4

NORTH SEA FISH PIE WITH SHRIMPS

Serves 4

1 lb (450 g) potatoes
1 lb (450 g) fillet of cod
2 hard-boiled eggs
1 teaspoonful mixed herbs
½ pint (300 ml/ 1¼ cups) shelled shrimps
A little fish liquid
A little butter and milk
Sliced tomato and chopped parsley to garnish

Peel and slice the potatoes and cook in salted water until soft.

Cook the fish gently in salted water for about 10 minutes.

Drain, retaining a little of the cooking liquid.

Skin the fish, and flake it into pieces, removing any bones.

Slice the hard-boiled eggs.

Mash the drained cooked potatoes with a knob of butter and a little milk, seasoning to taste, and beating the mixture well until light and fluffy.

Grease an ovenproof pie dish.

Arrange the flaked fish, hard-boiled egg, herbs and shrimps in the dish.

Pour on a little of the fish stock.

Cover the dish with mashed potato, fluffing the top up with a fork.

Dot the top with butter and bake in a moderate oven for about 20-30 minutes until well heated through and golden brown.

Serve hot, garnished with slices of tomato and chopped parsley.

Oven: 350°F/180°C Gas Mark 4

BERWICK-STYLE SALMON

This recipe comes from Ralph Holmes & Sons (fish merchants) in Bridge Street, Berwick-upon-Tweed, who have been established as a family business for over 200 years. The company has salmon netting stations on the River Tweed. They also have old fashioned smoke houses where the local salmon and trout are smoked.

1 cutlet of salmon per person
Salt
Melted butter
Cucumber to garnish

To cook salmon Berwick fashion:

First crimp the fish.

This means the fish is steaked and then the steaks are cut through the middle to make them chop-shaped.

Bring to the boil a saucepan or fish kettle (depending on the quantity of fish) containing well salted water.

Add the cutlets of fish and bring back to a fast boil.

Cook one minute to the pound of the weight of the original whole fish, even if only one portion is being cooked — if it was taken from a 7 lb salmon it must be boiled for seven minutes and if a whole cutletted fish which was originally 7 lbs in weight is being cooked it would still be boiled for only seven minutes.

Drain well, reserving some of the cooking liquid, which is called 'Dover'.

Garnish with cucumber, and serve with new potatoes and green peas.

MUSSELS IN WINE AND CREAM   Serves 4

Mussels have been gathered for food from the rocks round our shores for many centuries. It is known that the Romans enjoyed them during their occupation, and they were also eaten at medieval banquets. In Victorian times mussels and other shellfish such as cockles, whelks and winkles, were sold from stalls and by street criers. Mussel stews, similar to this, have been popular since the Middle Ages. They are in season from September to March.

6 pints (3.5 litres/15 cups) mussels
½ pint (300 ml/ 1¼ cups) water
2 medium onions
½ pint (300 ml/ 1¼ cups) dry white wine
2 oz (50 g) butter or margarine
1 oz (25 g) flour
¼ pint (150 ml/ ⅔ cup) milk
Salt and pepper
¼ pint (150 ml/ ⅔ cup) cream
1 oz (25 g) chopped parsley

Scrub and wash the mussels thoroughly, discarding any that will not close when tapped sharply.

Put the water in a saucepan and bring to the boil.

Add the mussels and simmer gently with the lid on the saucepan for 5 minutes or until all have opened.

Lift out the mussels and strain the liquid through a fine sieve and retain.

Remove the beard (a black strip used for breathing) from each mussel with a knife.

Take out the mussels from their shells, and keep hot.

Peel and chop the onions, and boil in the wine in an open saucepan until the liquid is reduced by half.

Melt the butter or margarine in a saucepan.

Stir in the flour to make a roux.

Gradually add the reduced wine, half the stock used to cook the mussels, and the milk.

Continue cooking and stirring until the sauce thickens.

Add the seasoning, cream and the chopped parsley.

Heat through thoroughly but do not allow the stew to boil again.

Arrange the mussels in a large serving dish or individual bowls. Pour on the sauce and serve hot.

HERRINGS IN OATMEAL WITH
MUSTARD SAUCE

Serves 6

Herrings are a small, oily fish caught round the shores of Northumberland. Obtainable all the year round, they are best from June to December. Herrings are inexpensive and a good source of first class protein. They are preserved as bloaters, kippers, red herrings, salt herrings and rollmops. Herring roes have a delicate flavour. Frying is an excellent way to get the full flavour of this delicious fish. Cooked to perfection, the oatmeal coating should be crisp, while the flesh remains moist.

For the herrings in oatmeal:
6 large or small herrings
About 4 oz (100g) fine oatmeal
Salt and pepper
Lemon wedges
Parsley
Oil for frying

To clean, gut and bone the fish:

Remove the head and the innards.

Take off any black skin by rubbing with salt, then wash well.

Scrape off the scales, and trim off the fins and tail.

Score the fish on both sides with a knife.

Split the herring completely up the stomach, from head to tail.

Spread the fish out on a board with the flesh side down.

Flatten the fish firmly by pressing it against the board, particularly along the backbone.

Turn the fish over and taking hold of one end of the backbone, pull it away. Most of the small bones will come away with the backbone.

To make the herrings in oatmeal:

Season the fish with salt and pepper.

Dip each fish into the oatmeal, pressing it on to both sides to give a good coating.

Heat the oil in a frying pan and fry the herrings, skin side first, for a total of about 8 minutes or until golden brown.

Do not allow the fat to get too hot or the oatmeal will burn, and the fish become dry.

Drain before serving, decorated with lemon wdges, parsley and accompanied with mustard sauce.

PRIZE WINNING BAKED HERRINGS

Serves 4

The prize winning secret of this recipe is the addition of a knob of best butter to each fish.

4 or 8 herrings, depending on appetite
Salt and pepper to taste
A little flour
A little butter

Clean, wash and fillet the herrings.

Place on a floured board with the skin side down.

Sprinkle the fish with salt, pepper and a little flour.

Put a knob of butter on each.

Roll up the herrings and put them in an ovenproof dish.

Pour on water to come three quarters of the way up the dish.

Bake for 1½ hours in a slow oven.

Oven: 300°F/150°C Gas Mark 2

PHEASANT IN LINDISFARNE MEAD

FROM RIVERDALE HALL

This dish has been created to feature the Northumberland specialities of game and Lindisfarne Mead, which is made on the Holy Island, by Iben Roust-Cocker, the Head Chef and joint proprietor with her husband, John, of the Riverdale Hall Hotel, at Bellingham, on the North Tyne river close to the Northumberland National Park and the Border Forest Park. The Victorian mansion was originally built in 1866 and the present owners bought it from Lord Stafford in 1979. Iben originates from the Danish capital of Copenhagen and is following in her Viking ancestor's footsteps by coming to Northumbria - but for a more peaceful purpose.

1 pheasant
½ bottle of Lindisfarne mead
1 small onion, finely chopped
2 oz (50 g) butter
1 teaspoon honey
1 bunch fresh chervil, finely chopped
4 juniper berries, crushed
5 fl. oz. (150 ml/ ⅔ cup) double cream
Salt and freshly milled black pepper

For the pheasant stock:
The bones and legs of the pheasant
3 bay leaves
The stalks of chervil and parsley
6 whole peppercorns
1 teaspoon salt
1 pint (600 ml/ 2½ cups) water

To make the pheasant stock:

Boil the bones with the herbs and seasoning in 1 pint of water for 1 hour.

To make the pheasant in mead:

Remove the pheasant breasts (or ask your butcher to do it, making sure to keep the bones).

Put the breasts in a deep dish and pour on the Lindisfarne mead, reserving 4 fl. oz (6 tablespoons/½ cup).

Cover the dish and store in the refrigerator for 24 hours turning the breasts a couple of times.

Sweat the onion in the butter in a deep frying pan.

Add the honey, chervil and juniper berries. Stir well.

Remove the breasts from the marinade (keep this on one side) and add them to the pan.

Fry the pheasant on both sides, making sure that the onions do not burn.

Add the 4 fl oz (300 ml/¼ cups) of pheasant stock - enough to cover the breasts.

Keep the pan on a brisk heat for about 7 minutes, turning the breasts from time to time.

Transfer the breasts to a plate and reduce the sauce to about one-third.

Turn down the heat and add the cream.

Boil up again for about 1 minute, adding the salt and pepper to taste.

Return the breasts briefly to the pan to heat through thoroughly before serving.

PIGEON PIE WITH BROWN ALE

For the pigeon pie:
2 pigeons (plucked and drawn)
8 oz (225 g) stewing beef
Pepper and salt to taste
1 pint (600 ml/ 2½ cups) brown ale
1 egg
¾ lb (350 g) shortcrust pastry

For the shortcrust pastry:
8 oz (225 g) self-raising flour
2 oz (50 g) lard
2 oz (50 g) margarine
A pinch of salt
Water to mix

To make the shortcrust pastry:

Sieve the flour.

Cut up the fat into small pieces.

Rub the fat into the flour until it resembles fine breadcrumbs.

Add the salt.

Mix with sufficient water to form a stiff dough.

Allow the pastry to rest for 30 minutes before rolling out on a floured board.

To make the pigeon pie:

Joint the birds into two breast joints and two leg joints each.

Cut the beef into small pieces and put in the bottom of a pie dish.

Lay the pigeon joints on top.

Cover with the brown ale.

Add the seasoning then cover the pie dish with a lid, and place it in a moderate oven to simmer for one hour.

Remove the dish from the oven.

Cover the pie with the shortcrust pastry.

Beat the egg and use to brush the top of the pie.

Return to the oven and bake until the pastry if golden brown.

Oven: 375°F/190°C Gas Mark 5

CITRUS FRUIT CHICKEN

Serves 4

FROM LANGLEY CASTLE

Langley Castle, now a luxurious hotel and restaurant, was built in 1350. Over the past 600 years the castle and its estates have been owned by many famous people associated with Northumbria's turbulent history. During the 17th century, it became the property of the Earls of Derwentwater. James, the third Earl and Charles his brother took part in the Jacobite risings of 1715 and were executed at the Tower of London.

The property was confiscated by the crown until 1882 when it was purchased by historian Cadweller Bates, who together with his wife Josephine, made the restoration of the Castle their life's work.

A 3 lb (1.5 kg) fresh chicken
½ orange
½ lime
½ lemon
Chicken stock
1 sprig of fresh tarragon
4 fl oz (6 tablespoons/½ cup) fresh double cream

Stuff the prepared chicken with the orange, lemon and lime.

Place the chicken in a deep casserole dish.

Half fill the dish with the chicken stock.

Add the fresh tarragon.

Cover with a tin foil lid.

Bake in a moderate oven for 2½ to 3 hours.

Boil the stock to reduce it by three quarters.

Stir in the fresh cream to finish.

Remove the chicken to a serving dish.

Serve the chicken with the sauce.

Oven: 350°F/180°C   Gas Mark 4

Reduce to: 350°F/180°C Gas Mark 4

CASSEROLE OF KIELDER VENISON IN
LINDISFARNE MEAD   Serves 4-6

2 lbs (900g) venison
2 oz (50 g) bacon fat
4 oz (100 g) mushrooms, chopped
1 cup of water
1 cup of Lindisfarne mead
2 onions
1 lb (450 g) potatoes
2 tablespoons plain flour
1 small teaspoon salt
¼ teaspoon paprika
A dash of black pepper

Mix the flour with the salt, paprika and black pepper.

Wipe the venison with a damp cloth, and cut into small pieces.

Rub the seasoning and flour mixture into each piece.

Heat the bacon fat to a moderate heat in a frying pan and fry the venison until brown on all sides.

Remove the meat to a casserole.

Add the water, Lindisfarne mead and chopped mushrooms.

Cook in a slow oven for about one and a half hours or until tender, removing the lid of the casserole for the last half hour of the cooking time.

Peel and chop the onions and fry until clear.

Peel, quarter and boil the potatoes.

Put the onions into the casserole and arrange the potatoes on top before serving.

Oven: 300°F/150°C Gas Mark 2

ROAST VENISON FROM
RABY CASTLE   Serves 8

It is believed that there have been herds of red and fallow deer roaming in the park at Raby Castle, Co. Durham, since before the Romans came to Britain. The first recorded owner of Raby was King Cnut, who, when he was King of Northumbria before becoming King of All England, had the nearby village of Staindrop as his provincial capital around 1020 AD. The present owner of the Castle is The Lord Barnard. Venison is not farmed at Raby; the venison comes from the estate, mostly from the woodland around the Castle. Since venison is a dense meat it becomes cold very quickly, so it must be served on very hot plates. The Victorians had special hot water dishes for serving it.

For the roast venison:
A haunch or shoulder of venison
Marinade
Flour and water paste, made with 1 lb (450 g) flour and
    ½ pint (300 ml/ 1¼ cups) water
3 - 4 oz (75 - 100g) softened (not melted) butter
Salt and pepper
Melted butter for basting
Gravy for game
Old Currant Sauce for Venison (see recipe)

For the marinade - sufficient for a shoulder or haunch:
2 glasses of red wine
3 tablespoons corn or other light cooking oil (not olive)
1 medium onion, sliced
1 dessertspoon juniper berries, crushed
1 teaspoon allspice
A bay leaf and parsley stalks

To marinate the venison:

Lay the meat in a deep china or glass dish (not metal).

Bring all the ingredients to the boil.

Allow to cool and pour over the meat.

22

Cover, and leave in a cool place for at least 24 hours preferably 2-3 days. Turn the meat occasionally and spoon the marinade over.

When required, remove the meat from the marinade and wipe carefully before roasting.

Strain the marinade and reserve to make the gravy.

To roast the venison:

Weigh the joint.

Mix the flour and water together to make a paste.

Roll out on a floured board to the required size to wrap round the joint.

Rub the joint with the salt, pepper and softened butter.

Encase the joint in the paste, making sure all the seams are sealed. Put in an unheated roasting tin in a hot oven.

Cook in a hot oven for 10 minutes. Reduce the heat to moderate and cook for 30 minutes for each lb (450g) of meat and 30 minutes over. Baste occasionally with melted butter.

Carefully remove the paste, reserving any liquid to add to the gravy.

Serve on a very hot dish with Gravy for Game and Old Currant Sauce.

Oven: 450°F/230°C Gas Mark 8
Reduce to: 350°F/180°C Gas Mark 4

GRAVY FOR GAME

½ pint (300 ml/ 1¼ cups) red wine
  (or the reserved marinade)
A teaspoon of anchovy essence or 2 strips of anchovy
1 shallot, chopped
½ pint (300 ml/ 1¼ cups) brown stock
½ teaspoon of ground black pepper
1 dessertspoon of flour
1 oz (25 g) butter
Wine or water if required

Cook all the ingrediants together, except the flour and butter, simmering the mixture gently for 1½ hours.

If the liquid reduces greatly, wine or water may be added as required.

Strain carefully.

Work the butter into the flour, and add this gradually to the liquid.

Beat well to avoid lumps and to thicken.

Serve separately in a sauceboat.

HUNTER'S RABBIT IN BEER

Serves 4

4 rabbit joints
4 rashers streaky bacon
2 onions
4 oz (100 g) mushrooms
Fat for frying
½ pint (300 ml/ 1¼ cups) beer
½ pint (300 ml/ 1¼ cups) water
Salt and pepper
1 oz (25 g) cornflour
2 tablespoons double cream

Trim, wash and dry the rabbit joints.

Remove the rind from the bacon and cut in into small pieces.

Peel and chop the onions.

Wash and slice the mushrooms.

Heat the fat in a frying pan and brown the rabbit joints on all sides. Remove and put into an ovenproof casserole.

Mix the beer and water together and pour over the casserole.

Season with salt and pepper.

Cover the casserole and cook in a moderate oven for 2 hours.

Blend the cornflour with a little cold water to make a smooth paste.

Remove the casserole from the oven and stir in the cornflour.

Return to the oven and cook for a further 5 minutes.

Stir in the cream just before cooking.

Oven: 325°F/160°C Gas Mark 3

DURHAM BEEF WITH SUET DUMPLINGS

Serves 4 -5

Durham Castle has a medieval kitchen (which is still used today.) It was first converted from the original Norman guardsroom nearly 500 years ago.

For the beef casserole:
1½ lbs (675 g) stewing steak
2 onions
4 carrots
Salt and Pepper
A little flour
Fat for frying
1 pint (600 ml/ 2½ cups) brown stock

For the suet dumplings: (makes 4 dumplings)
4 oz (100 g) self-raising flour
A little extra flour
2 oz (50 g) shredded or chopped suet
A pinch of salt and pepper
Milk or cold water to mix

To make the beef casserole:

Cut the meat into small pieces, discarding any fat.

Peel and slice the onions and carrots.

Mix the salt and pepper with the flour and use to coat the meat.

Melt the fat in a frying pan.

Fry the meat to seal on all sides.

Remove and put in a casserole dish.

Fry the onions until soft.

Add to the casserole with the sliced carrots.

Pour on the stock, and season with salt and pepper to taste.

Cover the casserole with a lid.

Cook in a moderate oven for about 1¾ hours, before the dumplings are added, or 2 hours if the dumplings are omitted.

To make the suet dumplings:

Sieve the flour.

Stir in the salt and suet.

Mix well, and add sufficient milk or water to make into a soft dough.

Form into balls with floured hands.

Drop into the casserole, and continue cooking for a further 15-20 minutes until the dumplings are light and fluffy.

GRANNY'S POT PIE

This is one of the many varieties of the classic British steak and kidney pudding, one of the best known and oldest of savoury puddings. Puddings today can be either sweet or savoury. The very first puddings were made using a number of savoury items boiled in the stomach bag of an animal.

8 oz (225 g) self-raising flour
½ teaspoonful salt
3 oz (75 g) shredded suet
A little water
1 lb (450 g) stewing steak
8 oz (225 g) kidney
Salt and pepper
A little extra flour
½ pint (300 ml/ 1¼ cups) brown stock

Mix the flour, salt and suet together with cold water to make a stiff dough.

Roll out the pastry on a floured board, and use three quarters to line a 1 pint (600 ml/ 2½ cups) greased pudding basin.

Cut up the beef and kidney into small pieces.

Season a little flour with salt and pepper, and roll the meat in it.

Put the meat into the basin.

Pour the stock over the meat.

Use the remainder of the pastry to make a lid.

Dampen the edges of the pastry and place the lid on top of the pudding, pressing the edges firmly together to join.

Prick the top of the pudding to allow the steam to escape.

Cover the pudding with a foil lid or pudding cloth, tie down securely, and steam for 3 hours.

Turn out the pudding to serve.

TATTIE STOVIES

Serves 6

Left-over cooked meat or bacon
2 lb (900g) potatoes
2 onions
2 oz (50 g) beef dripping or butter
Salt and pepper
½ pint (300 ml/ 1¼ cups) stock

Cut up the meat into small pieces.

Peel and slice the potatoes and onions.

Melt the dripping or butter in a saucepan.

Cook the onions slightly in hot fat.

Add the potatoes.

Season with salt and pepper.

Add the stock.

Bring slowly to the boil, cover the pan and simmer gently for about three quarters of an hour, stirring occasionally to prevent the mixture sticking.

Stir in the cut up meat, continue cooking for a further 15 minutes until all the liquid is absorbed.

Put in a pie dish and brown in a hot oven before serving.

SARAH'S PIE

This is the recipe of Sarah Smith, a servant girl, who worked in the house of Sir Arthur Sutherland, a large ship owner in the north east at the turn of the century.

When Sir Arthur's cook was ill, young Sarah had to take over her duties. The result of her first attempt was a delicious pie which Sir Arthur appropriately christened Sarah's Pie. As a reward, Sarah Smith remained as cook in Sir Arthur's home for many years.

12 oz (350 g) stewing beef
4 oz (100 g) ox or lamb kidney
8 oz (225 g) ham
Beef stock
4 slices of black pudding
A little flour or cornflour
4 eggs, hard-boiled and peeled
Shortcrust pastry
Beaten egg to glaze

Dice the meat and place in a deep pie dish.

Add enough beef stock to just cover the meat.

Cook in a mdoerate oven for about 1½ hours, until the meat is tender.

Remove from the oven, and thicken the stock if necessary with a little flour or cornflour.

Add the black pudding and hard-boiled eggs.

Roll out the pastry to slightly larger than the size of the pie dish.

Cut off a strip of pastry, damp the edge of the pie dish and lay the pastry strip around the edge.

Cover with the remaining pastry.

Press down the edges.

Trim off the surplus pastry and flute the edges.

Use the pastry trimmings to make leaves to decorate the top.

Brush with beaten egg.

Place in a hot oven and bake for about 25 minutes until the pastry is golden brown.

Serve hot or cold.

Oven: 325°F/180°C Gas Mark 3
Increase to 400°C/200°C Gas Mark 6

TATTIE POT OR MUTTON AND POTATO PIE

Serves 6

6 middle neck lamb chops
3 lambs kidneys
2 black puddings or to taste
8 oz (225 g) onions
1½ lbs (675 g) potatoes
Salt and pepper
½ pint (300 ml/ 1¼ cups) white stock - to give the
   traditional light colour
1 oz (25 g)dripping or lard

Trim any excess fat from the chops.

Skin and remove the core from the kidneys, and slice.

Slice the black pudding.

Peel and slice the potatoes and onions.

Fry the chops and kidneys on both sides in a frying pan in their own fat for a few minutes.

Put the chops in an overproof casserole.

Cover the chops with a layer of kidney, black pudding, onions and potatoes, seasoning each layer with salt and pepper.

Continue with the layers, until all the ingredients are used, finishing with a layer of potatoes.

Pour on the stock.

Melt the dripping or lard in a saucepan.

Brush the potatoes over with the melted fat.

Cover the casserole with a lid or foil and bake in a moderate oven for 2 hours.

Remove the lid, and brown the potatoes for a further 20 minutes in a hot oven.

Oven: 325°F/160°F Gas Mark 3
Increase to: 425°F/220°C Gas Mark 7

OLD NAN'S DURHAM PANACKLETY

1 large onion
4 potatoes
8 rashers of bacon
4 oz (100 g) pig's liver
4 tablepoons water
Flour and salt for dredging

Peel and chop the onion.

Peel and slice the potatoes.

Put half the chopped onion, half the sliced potatoes, 4 rashers of bacon and 2 oz (50 g) of pig's liver in layers in a shallow casserole dish.

Repeat the layers again.

Pour on the water and dredge the dish with flour and salt.

Cook in a moderate oven for 25-30 minutes.

Oven: 350°F/180°C Gas Mark 4

NORTHUMBERLAND PANJOTHERAM

Serves 4

This tasty casserole of lamb chops and potatoes is known by the local name of panjotheram.

1 lb (450 g) potatotes
2 onions
Salt and pepper to taste
4 lamb or mutton chops
A little fat for frying
1 oz (25 g) flour
½ pint (300 ml/ 1¼ cups) brown stock

Peel and slice the potatoes and onions.

Put the potatoes and onions in layers in a casserole dish.

Season each layer with salt and pepper to taste.

Heat the fat in a frying pan, and lightly fry the chops on both sides to seal.

Remove the chops, and arrange them in the casserole on top of the vegetables.

Stir the flour into the fat in the frying pan.

Gradually add the stock, still stirring, and bring to the boil.

Pour the hot stock over the casserole.

Cover the casserole with a lid or foil.

Cook in a moderate oven for about 1 hour or until tender.

Oven:350°F/180°C   Gas Mark 4

ALNWICK STEW

Serves 6

This tasty bacon stew originates from Alnwick, a walled town in Northumberland. Starting in 1433 it took 50 years to build the walls. Alnwick, as the centre of a prosperous agricultural region has at one time its own courts and rules relating to fairs and guilds. The town held its first market in 1291, and has always been an important centre for surrounding villages. The Percy family - the Earls and Dukes of Northumberland - has made its home at Alnwick Castle since the 14th century. Alnwick is on the old coaching route from London to Edinburgh, and its many ancient inns have always offered warm hospitality to the traveller.

2 lb (900 g) bacon - forelock or collar
2 lb (900 g) potatoes
1 lb (450 g) onions
Pepper
About 2 pints (1.15 litres/ 5 cups) water

Cut the bacon into cubes.

Peel and slice the potatoes.

Peel and slice the potatoes.

Peel and slice the onions.

Put layers of the meat and vegetables in an ovenproof dish, seasoning each layer with pepper. Finish with a layer of overlapping potatoes.

Pour on enough water to come just below the final layer of potatoes.

Cover the dish with a lid and cook in a moderate oven for about 1½ hours.

Remove the lid for the last 30 minutes of the cooking time to brown the potatoes.

Oven: 350°F/180°C Gas Mark 4

PATTY TOPPERS

1½ lbs (675 g) potatoes
1 onion
8 oz (225 g) cooked meat
Salt and pepper
1 oz (25 g) butter
Fat for frying
8 eggs (optional)

Peel and cut up the potatoes.

Put into a saucepan of cold water, bring to the boil, then simmer until cooked.

Mash the potatoes until smooth.

Peel and chop the onion.

Cut the meat into small pieces.

Add the meat, onion, seasoning and butter to the potatoes.

Put the mixture on a floured board, and form into eight round cakes or patties.

Heat the fat in a frying pan.

Fry the patties until golden brown on both sides.

For a complete meal, serve with a fried egg on top of each patty.

PAN HAGGERTY

This traditional Northumberland recipe, which was originally made from left-overs, but is certainly worthy of making from fresh ingredients, makes a delicious lunch, supper or high tea snack.

1 lb (450 g) potatoes
8 oz (225 g) onions
4 oz (100 g) cheese
2 oz (50 g) butter or dripping
Salt and pepper

Peel and cut the potatoes into thin slices.

Peel and thinly slice the onions.

Grate the cheese.

Heat the butter or dripping in a heavy flameproof pan.

Put layers of potatoes, onion and cheese into the pan, seasoning each layer with salt and pepper, and finishing with a layer of potatoes.

Cover the pan with a lid, and cook very slowly on top of the stove for about 40 minutes, until the potatoes are tender.

Brown the potatoes under a hot grill for a few minutes before serving straight from the pan.

LEEK PUDDING
(WITH BACON OR MINCE)

Serves 3 - 4

1½ lbs (675 g) leeks
8 oz (225 g) plain flour
A pinch of salt
2 teaspoons baking powder
3 oz (75 g) shredded suet
¼ pint (150 ml/ ⅔ cup) cold water
A little milk
Optional extra: 8 oz (225 g) chopped bacon or 8 oz
  (225 g) cooked mince

Sieve the flour, salt and baking powder into a bowl.

Stir in the suet and beat in the water to form a light dough, adding extra water if necessary.

Roll out to a rectangular shape ¼ inch (1 cm) thick.

Wash and finely slice the leeks and dry throroughly.

Spread the leeks over the dough mix.

If using an optional filling, sprinkle it over the leeks.

Dampen the edges of the dough mix with milk.

Roll up to form a swiss roll shape.

Press the edges to seal.

Put into a saucepan half filled with hot water, and steam over a low heat for about 2½ hours, ensuring that the pan does not boil dry.

LEEK PUDDING - ANOTHER WAY   Serves 4

For the leek pudding:
6 leeks
1 lb (450 g) savoury suet pastry
3 oz (75 g) butter
Salt and pepper to taste

For the savoury suet pastry:
8 oz (225 g) plain flour
4 oz (100 g) chopped suet
A pinch of salt
¼ pint (150 ml/ ⅔ cup) cold water

To make the savoury suet pastry:

Mix the flour, suet and salt together with the cold water to make a stiff dough.

To make the leek pudding:

Trim, wash and chop the leeks.

Roll out the pastry on a floured board, and use three quarters to line a 2 pints (1.15 litres/ 5 cups) greased pudding basin.

Pack the leeks tightly into the basin, seasoning each layer with salt and pepper to taste.

Cut the butter into small pieces and use to dot the leeks.

Make a lid with the remaining pastry. Place the lid on the pudding.

Dampen the pastry edges, pressing the edges firmly together to join.

Cover the pudding with a foil lid or pudding cloth, and tie down securely.

Steam for 2 hours.

Turn out to serve.

LEEK AND GOOSE EGG FLAN

Every year for centuries the Ovingham Goose Fair has been held on the third Saturday in June. At the start of festivities, which are held in honour of the Duke of Northumberland, tenants and visitors are led through the streets by a Northumbrian piper and Morris dancers. Sword dancing is also a feature of the Fair.

In the 5th century, Ovingham, a village in the middle Tyne valley, was an encampment. Flocks of geese were kept as guards. Their eggs, which were used then to help feed the Roman troops, are still used today to make delicious egg and leak flan.

For the shortcrust pastry:
8 oz (225 g) plain flour, sieved
4 oz (100 g) margarine
2 tablespoons cold water

For the goose egg filling:
1 oz (25 g) margarine
1 large leek, washed and sliced
2 sticks celery, washed and chopped
2 oz (50 g) mushrooms, sliced and sautéed in a little margarine
1 oz (25 g) flour
¼ pint (150 ml/ ⅔ cup) milk or cream
¼ pint (150 ml/ ⅔ cup) white wine
1 tablespoon chopped parsley
1 goose egg, beaten
Salt and black pepper

To make the pastry:

Place the flour in a bowl and rub in the margarine until the mixture resembles fine breadcrumbs.

Add the water and mix to a firm dough.

Knead gently until smooth.

Roll out on a lightly floured surface to a round large enough to line a 7-8 inch (18-20 cm) flan dish.

Line the dish with the pastry and trim the edges.

Leave in a cool place for 15 minuted to 'relax'.

Bake 'blind' in a hot oven for 15 minutes.

Remove the baking beans.

Oven: 400°F/200°C Gas Mark 6

To make the leek and goose egg filling:

Melt the margarine over a gentle heat and sauté the leek and celery for a few minutes.

Add the flour and stir over the heat for 1 minute.

Add the milk and wine gradually, stirring continuously.

Bring to the boil and boil for 1 minute.

Add the parsley, egg and seasoning.

Place the mushrooms in the bottom of the flan case, reserving a few for decoration.

Pour over the leek and celery mixture.

Bake in the centre of the oven for about 30 minutes.

Garnish with the remaining mushrooms.

Oven: 350°F/180°C Gas Mark 4

LEEK AND POTATO SAVOURY   Serves 4

This savoury is excellent as a supper dish or as an accompaniment to meat, especially pork chops or boiled bacon.

1 lb (450 g) leeks
1 lb (450 g) potatoes
3 oz (75 g) cheese
Salt and pepper
1 egg
½ pint (300 ml/ 1¼ cups) milk

Trim, wash and slice the leeks.

Peel and slice the potatoes.

Grate the cheese.

Put a layer of potatoes in the bottom of a fireproof dish.

Sprinkle the potatoes with cheese and seasoning to taste.

Put a layer of leeks on top, and sprinkle with cheese and seasoning.

Continue in this fashion until all the vegetables are used up, finishing with a sprinkling of cheese.

Beat the egg into the milk, and pour on to the dish.

Bake in a moderate oven for 1 hour or until golden brown and the potatoes are tender.

Oven: 350°F/180°C Gas Mark 4

CELERY CHEESE

Serves 3 - 4

1 head of celery
Salt and pepper
A little milk
3 oz (75 g) hard cheese
1 egg
Breadcrumbs for topping
A little butter

Prepare the celery, and grate it or chop very finely.

Put into a saucepan.

Pour on enough milk to just cover the vegetable.

Season with salt and pepper.

Simmer gently for about 10 minutes or until the celery is tender.

While the mixture is cooling, grate the cheese and beat the egg.

Mix the cheese and egg into the celery.

Put the mixture into a greased ovenproof dish.

Cover the top with breadcrumbs.

Cut up the butter into small pieces and use to dot the top of the breadcrumbs.

Bake in a moderate oven for about 15 minutes until golden brown

Oven: 350°F/180°C Gas Mark 4

CARLINS

Carlins are dried pulses. They can be obtained in specialist grocer's shops and on market stalls. Traditionally they were served in the home and also in pubs on Passion Sunday, the fifth Sunday after Lent, which became known as 'Carlin Sunday'.

8 oz (225 g) carlins
2 oz (50 g) butter
Salt and pepper to taste
A little vinegar

Soak the carlins overnight in water, then strain.

Put in a saucepan, cover with water and bring to the boil.

Simmer for about 20 minutes until soft, then strain.

Melt the butter in a saucepan, and add the carlins.

Fry for a few minutes.

Serve hot, seasoned with salt and pepper, and sprinkled with a dash of vinegar.

PEASE PUDDING

Traditionally pease pudding or porridge as it was first called, was served with boiled, salted or pickled pork. Pease pudding was sold by street vendors until the last century.

8 oz (225 g) split peas
Salt and pepper
1 oz (25 g) butter or margarine
1 egg

Wash the peas well, and remove any black ones.

Soak in cold water overnight.

Put in a cloth, and tie it loosely allowing plenty or room for the peas to swell.

Plunge into a saucepan containing enough boiling salted water to cover the bag.

Boil for 2 hours or until the peas are soft.

Lift the bag out of the water, and rub the peas through a sieve or purée in an electric blender.

Beat the egg.

Stir in the butter, egg and salt and pepper to taste.

Beat until thoroughly mixed.

Tie up the pudding tightly in a floured cloth and boil for a further 30 minutes.

If the dish is to be eaten with boiled pork, bacon or any boiled meat, put the pudding in with the meat for the second boiling, as the broth will improve the flavour.

If the pease pudding is to be served without boiled meat, the second boiling can be in water.

Chopped onion and mint may be added for additional flavour with the butter, egg and seasoning.

Turn on to a hot plate to serve.

EGGS IN A BED

2 oz (50 g) butter
4 oz (100 g) mushrooms
2 tomatoes
Salt
Black pepper
4 oz (100 g) Cheddar cheese
4 eggs
4 tablespoons single cream or top of the milk
Parsley, chopped

Peel and slice the mushrooms.

Skin and chop the tomatoes.

Grate the cheese.

Melt the butter in a frying pan.

Fry the mushrooms and tomatoes for a few minutes.

Season to taste.

Grease four individual fireproof dishes.

Put equal quanitities of the mixture into each dish.

Leave half the grated cheese on one side.

From the remaining 2 oz (50 g) put an equal quantity into each dish on top of the vegetables.

Break an egg into each dish.

Gently pour one tablespoon of cream over each egg.

Top each portion with the remaining cream.

Bake in a moderate oven for 8-10 minutes, until the eggs are set and the cheese has melted.

Serve immediately, garnished with the chopped parsley.

Oven: 350°F/180°C Gas Mark 4

WHITLEY GOOSE

An old Northumberland dish made of cheese and onions, not from goose.

4 large onions
12 oz (350 g) hard cheese
6 oz (175 g) fresh breadcrumbs
Salt and pepper
¼ pint (150 ml/ ⅔ cup) milk
1 oz (25 g) butter

Peel and slice the onions.

Grate the cheese.

Put layers of cheese, onions and breadcrumbs in a fireproof dish, seasoning each layer with salt and pepper to taste.

Reserve some cheese and breadcrumbs.

Pour on the milk.

Finish with a layer of cheese topped with breadcrumbs and sprinkled with a little more cheese.

Cut the butter into small pieces and use to dot on the top of the cheese.

Bake in a moderate oven for about 40 minutes, until the onion is cooked, and the top crisp and brown.

Oven: 350°F/180°C Gas Mark 4

BILBERRY PIE

Bilberrys grow wild on the moorlands. They used to be gathered in the summer, and used in pies and puddings.

For the bilberry pie:
1 lb (450 g) bilberries
2 baked cooking apples
8 oz (225 g) sugar
12 oz (350 g) sweet shortcrust pastry
1 egg
2 fl oz (3 tablespoons/¼ cup) double cream
A little caster sugar

For the sweetcrust pastry:
8 oz (225 g) self-raising flour
4 oz (100 g) butter or margarine
1 oz (25 g) sugar
Cold water to mix

To make the sweetcrust pastry:

Sieve the flour into a bowl.

Cut up the fat and rub it into the flour until it resembles fine breadcrumbs.

Add the sugar.

Mix with sufficient cold water to give a stiff dough.

Allow the pastry to rest for 30 minutes before using.

To bake the apples:

Remove the cores with an apple corer.

Stand the apples in an ovenproof dish.

Add 2 tablespoon of water to the dish.

Bake in a moderate oven for 45 minutes until tender.

To make the bilberry pie.

Scrape the pulp from the baked apples and mix with the bilberries and sugar.

Roll our half of the sweetcrust pastry on a floured board and use to line a greased 8 inch pie plate.

Cover the pastry with the fruit mixture and dampen the edges with a little water.

Roll out the rest of the pastry to make a lid.

Put the lid on the pie and press the edges together to seal.

Make a slit in the centre of the pie for the steam to escape.

Beat the egg white and use to brush over the top of the pie.

Sprinkle with a little caster sugar.

Bake in a hot oven for 10 minutes and then at a moderate heat for 30 minutes until golden brown.

When baked, lift up the top crust and pour in the thick cream.

Delicious served hot or cold.

Oven: 400°F/200°C Gas Mark 6 for the baked apples

Oven: 425°F/220°C Gas Mark 7 for 10 minutes for
      bilberry pie
Reduce to: 350°/180°C Gas Mark 4 for 30 minutes

JOHN PEEL TART

4 oz (100 g) golden syrup
1 oz (25 g) butter
6 oz (175 g) currants
1 dessertspoon lemon juice
½ teaspoon mixed spice
1 oz (25 g) ground almonds
8 oz (225 g) shortcrust pastry

Put the syrup and butter in a saucepan.

Stir over a low heat until melted.

Remove from the heat and mix in the currants, lemon juice, mixed spice and almonds.

Roll out half the pastry and use to line a shallow oblong baking tin.

Spread the mixture on the pastry.

Roll out the rest of the pastry and use to cover the mixture.

Bake in a moderately hot oven for 40 minutes or until golden brown.

Cut into squares to serve.

Oven: 400°F/200°C Gas Mark 6

BREAD AND BUTTER PUDDING   Serves 4

4 or 5 thin slices of white bread and butter
2 oz (50 g) sultanas or raisins
1 oz (25 g) caster sugar
½ pint (300 ml/ 1¼ cups) milk
2 eggs
Vanilla flavouring (optional)
Ground nutmeg
Whipped cream to serve

Cut the bread into quarters.

Arrange the bread, butter side up in layers in a greased pie dish, sprinkling each layer with the dried fruit and sugar.

Gently heat the milk in a saucepan, but do not allow it to boil.

Whisk the eggs together in a bowl.

Pour the milk on to the eggs, stirring.

Flavour with a little vanilla, if liked.

Pour the milk mixture over the bread.

Leave to stand for 15 minutes.

Dust the top of the pudding with ground nutmeg.

Bake in a moderate oven for 30-45 minutes or until set and lightly brown.

Serve with whipped cream.

Oven:350°F/180°C Gas Mark 4

NEWCASTLE PUDDING WITH LEMON SAUCE

Serves 4

The walled city of Newcastle is the capital of the north east. An important city, its prosperity throughout its long history has been based on wool, coal, salt, lime and glass making, and since the 19th century on shipbuilding and railways as well. Newcastle became a leading port because of its location on the river Tyne. Fruit and spices have long been imported into the port for distribution throughout the north of England.

This is another favourite way of making bread and butter pudding — with a lemony flavour.

1 pint (600 ml/ 2½ cups) milk
1 lemon
3 eggs
2 oz (50 g) caster sugar
About 6 slices of bread
A little butter

Warm the milk in a saucepan in blood heat.

Remove from the stove.

Grate the lemon rind finely and add it to the milk.

Leave the mixture to stand for at least 1 hour.

Beat the eggs in a basin and whisk the sugar into the egg mixture.

Pour on the milk, and mix to make a custard.

Butter the bread, and remove the crusts.

Carefully line a greased 1½ pint (1 litre) pudding basin with the slices of bread.

Pour on the custard mixture and leave the pudding to stand for another hour.

Cover with greaseproof paper and a foil lid.

Tie down securely.

Put the basin in a saucepan of boiling water, cover and steam for 45 minutes to 1 hour, topping the water up in the saucepan if necessary.

Turn out onto a dish and serve with Lemon Sauce (see recipe).

RHUBARB PUDDING

Serves 4

Rhubarb, a popular fruit in the north, is grown by many people in gardens or on allotments.

3 oz (75 g) demerara sugar
1 lb (450 g) rhubarb
About 8 slices of white bread about ¼" (5 mm) thick
A little milk
About 2 oz (50 g) butter

Grease the bottom and sides of a 1 pint (600 ml / 2½ cups) pudding basin.

Sprinkle demerara sugar fairly thickly on the bottom.

Peel the rhubarb and cut it into 1" (2.5 cm) pieces.

Cut the crusts off the bread.

Dampen the bread with the milk, but do not allow it to become very wet.

Neatly line the bottom and sides of the basin with some of the bread so that there are no gaps.

Reserve slices of bread for the lid, and for layers between the fruit.

Put a layer of rhubarb in the basin, and sprinkle with demerara sugar to taste.

Put a slice of bread on top of the fruit.

Dot the bread with small knobs of butter.

Continue with layers of fruit and bread as before until the basin is full.

Finish with a layer of bread shaped to form a neat-fitting lid.

Sprinkle the top well with demerara sugar and dot with butter.

Tie the pudding securely down with a cloth or foil lid.

Steam for 1 hour.

Turn the pudding out of the basin and serve with cream or custard.

GINGER SPONGE PUDDING

4 oz (100 g) self-raising flour
2½ oz (65 g) sugar
1 teaspoon ground ginger
4 tablespoons milk
2 oz (50 g) margarine
1 dessertspoon golden syrup
½ teaspoon bicarbonate of soda
Extra syrup for sauce when serving

Mix the flour, sugar and ginger together.

Put the milk, margarine and syrup into a saucepan.

Bring to the boil and stir in the bicarbonate of soda.

Add the flour, sugar and ginger, and mix all well together.

Put the mixture into a well greased ovenproof dish.

Bake in a moderate oven for 30 minutes.

Serve with extra syrup poured over the pudding.

Oven: 325°F/160°C Gas Mark 3

SPOTTED DICK

Serves 4

This popular pudding is also known as Spotted Dog. It gets its name from the dried fruit in the suet dough.

8 oz (225 g) self-raising flour
4 oz (100 g) shredded suet
2 oz (50 g) sugar
4 oz (100 g) currants
A little milk to mix
Brown sugar, custard or sweet white sauce to serve

Sieve the flour into a bowl.

Stir in the shredded suet, sugar and currants.

Make a well in the centre, and add enough milk to give a fairly stiff dough.

Turn the mixture on to a floured board, and shape it into a roll.

Wrap the pudding loosely in greaseproof paper and then tie in a floured cloth or tin foil leaving room for expansion.

Steam or boil for 1½ hours.

Alternatively add enough milk to make the mixture of a soft dropping consistency.

Put it into a greased 1½ pint (900 ml/ 3¾ cups) pudding basin.

Tie down well and steam for 1½ hours.

Unwrap or turn out the pudding on to a warm serving dish.

Serve sprinkled with brown sugar and accompanied by custard or a sweet white sauce.

MINCE PIES

8 oz (225 g) rose pastry (see recipe)
8 oz (225 g) mincemeat
1 egg
A little caster or icing sugar

Roll out the pastry on a lightly floured surface.

Cut out 12 rounds with a 2½″ (6 cm) cutter and 12 rounds with a 2″ (5 cm) cutter.

Grease 12 patty tins.

Line the patty tins with the larger rounds.

Fill each with a teaspoonful of mincemeat.

Dampen the edges with water.

Cover with the remaining pastry rounds.

Press the edges together to seal.

Make a small slit in the top of each pie.

Brush with beaten egg.

Bake in a hot oven for about 20 minutes until golden brown.

Remove from the oven.

Dust with caster sugar whilst still hot or allow to cool and dredge with icing sugar before serving.

Oven: 400°F/200°C Gas Mark 6

Served hot or cold.

SWEET ROSE PASTRY

Makes approximately 12-14 oz (350-400 g) pastry

Excellent for making mince pies.

9 oz (250 g) self-raising flour
2 oz (50 g) cornflour
2 oz (50 g) icing sugar
5 oz (150 g) margarine
Cold water to mix

Sieve the flour and cornflour into a basin.

Stir in the icing sugar.

Cut up the margarine into small pieces.

Rub ·the fat into the mixture until it resembles fine breadcrumbs.

Mix the enough cold water to make a stiff dough.

Allow the pastry to rest, preferably in a refrigerator, for 30 minutes before use.

Roll out as required.

DURHAM POPOVERS

Makes 6 popovers

Popovers are an individual batter pudding. They are traditionally served plain with roast beef, but can be made with savoury or sweet alternatives. Popular additions to the basic mixture to serve for high tea or supper are a little grated cheese, chopped onion, bacon or herbs. Chopped fruit, such as apples, may be added to the basic batter to make a delicious sweet popover, or the plain version can be served with jam or syrup as pudding.

4 oz (100 g) plain flour
A pinch of salt
1 egg
½ pint (300 ml/ 1¼ cups) milk

Sieve the flour and salt into a bowl.

Make a well in the centre and break the egg into it.

Gradually add half the milk, a little at a time, mixing with a wooden spoon, and gradually drawing in the flour to make a smooth batter.

Stir in the remainder of the milk.

Two thirds fill six well greased patty tins with the mixture.

Bake in a hot oven for 20 to 30 minutes until well risen, nicely brown, and light and hollow inside.

Remove from the patty tins, and serve very hot.

Oven: 425°F/220°C Gas Mark 7

DARK GINGERBREAD

There are various types of gingerbread made throughout Great Britain.

8 oz (225 g) self-raising flour
4 oz (100 g) butter or margarine
4 oz (100 g) moist brown sugar
1 teaspoon ground ginger
1 pinch of mixed spice
2 tablespoons treacle or golden syrup
1 level teaspoon bicarbonate of soda
2 eggs
1 teacup ¼ pint (150 ml/ ⅔ cup) milk

Sieve the flour.

Rub the butter or margarine into the flour until the mixture resembles fine breadcrumbs.

Stir in the sugar, ginger and spice.

Warm the milk and dissolve the treacle in it.

Stir in the bicarbonate of soda into the liquid.

Add to the mixture with the beaten eggs.

Mix altogether to give a soft dropping consistency.

Put in a greased tin.

Bake in a moderate oven for 30-40 minutes.

Oven: 350°F/180°C Gas Mark 4

QUICK GINGER SPONGE PARKIN

Ginger parkins are traditional in the north of England. This recipe comes from Netherton.

2 oz (50 g) margarine
A pinch of salt
5 oz (150 g) sugar
1 large egg
1 dessertspoon golden syrup
8 oz (225 g) self-raising flour
2 gently rounded teaspoons ground ginger
1 level teaspoon bicarbonate of soda
A little milk to mix

Put the margarine, salt, sugar, egg and syrup into a mixing bowl.

In a separate bowl, mix the flour and ginger together.

Add the flour and ginger to the other ingredients.

Mix all together well with a little milk.

Thoroughly stir in the bicarbonate of soda.

Put in a greased tin.

Bake in a moderate oven for 45 minutes to 1 hour.

Oven: 350°F/180°C Gas Mark 4

COTTAGE TEATIME CAKE

½ pint (300 ml/ 1¼ cups) tea
4 oz (100 g) butter
5 oz (150 g) soft brown sugar
10 oz (275 g) self-raising flour
4 oz (100 g) currants
6 oz (175 g) sultanas
2 level teaspoons mixed spice
1 large egg

Put the tea, butter and brown sugar in a saucepan.

Bring to the boil, then simmer for 20 minutes, stirring occasionally.

Remove the saucepan from the heat, and allow the mixture to cool.

Sieve the flour, and stir it into the mixture, together with the dried fruit, spice and lightly beaten egg.

Mix well.

Put the mixture into a greased tin.

Bake in a moderate oven for 1 hour 15 minutes.

Oven: 350°F/180°C Gas Mark 4

BIBLE CAKE

This is a delicious cake, which was very popular in the north country, particularly at the end of the last century. The ingredients for the recipe, which has been handed down through the generations, will be found by reading the Bible.

1. ½ lb Judges 5, v.25
2. ½ lb Jeremiah 6, v.20   *SUGAR*
3. 1 tablespoon 1 Samuel 14, v.25 *HONEY*
4. 3 of Jermiah 17, v.11   *EGGS*
5. ½ lb 1 Samuel 30, v.12
6. ½ lb Nahum 3, v.12 (chopped)
7. 2 oz Numbers 17, v.8 (blanched and chopped)
8. 1 lb 1 Kings 4, v.22
9. Season to taste with 2 Chronicles 9, v.9
10. A pinch of Leviticus 2, v.13
11. A teaspoon of Amos 4, v.5
12. 3 tablespoons Judges 4, v.19

Beat 1, 2 and 3 to a cream.

Add 4, one at a time.

Add 5, 6 and 7. Beat again.

Then add 8, 9, 10 and 11, having previously mixed them.

Add 12.

Bake in a moderate oven for 1½ hours.

63

TWELFTH NIGHT OR BEAN CAKE

In the Middle Ages it was customary to bake a large flat cake made of flour, sugar, ginger, pepper, eggs and dried fruit to celebrate the season of Twelvetide or Epiphany. A whole dried bean was hidden in the cake to bring good luck. The finder was crowned king or queen of the celebrations, which were known as a Bean Feast. The cake is traditionally covered with royal icing, and decorated with glacé cherries, and citron cut into fancy shapes. Red sugar candle holders with lighted candles add the final festive touch. This rich fruit cake is also suitable to make for other festivals, such as birthdays, Christmas or Easter.

8 oz (225 g) butter
8 oz (225 g) soft brown sugar
4 eggs
8 oz (225 g) plain flour
A pinch of salt
½ teaspoon of ground cinnamon
½ teaspoon of ground ginger
½ teaspoon of allspice
8 oz (225 g) currants
8 oz (225 g) sultanas
4 oz (100 g) almonds, blanched and chopped
4 oz (100 g) mixed chopped candied peel
2 fl oz (3 tablespoons/ ¼ cup) orange juice or
   2 fl oz (3 tablespoons/¼ cup) brandy
2½ lbs (1.25 kg) marzipan
Royal icing
Glacé cherries or citron to decorate

To make the cake:

Cream the butter and sugar until light and fluffy.

Beat in the eggs a little at a time, beating well after each addition.

Sieve the flour, salt and spices.

Fold in half the flour, then fold in the remainder with the orange juice or brandy.

Fold in the dried fruit, peel and almonds to give a soft dropping consistency.

Put the mixture in a greased 8 inch (20 cm) cake tin, double lined with greaseproof paper.

Make a dip in the centre of the mixture.

Bake in a slow oven for 3 hours.

For the marzipan:
1 lb 2 oz (500 g) ground almonds
9 oz (250 g) icing sugar, sieved
9 oz (250 g) caster sugar
4 large egg whites
¼ teaspoon of almond essence
Some melted apricot jam

To make the marzipan:

Mix all the ingredients together thoroughly.

Knead the mixture into a paste.

Divide the marzipan into two.

To put the marzipan on the cake:

Roll out one piece on a floured board to fit the top of the cake. Measure round the side of the cake with a piece of string, and cut off the measured length.

Roll out the other piece of marzipan to the depth of the cake and the length of the piece of string.

Brush the side of the cake with the melted jam, and fit on the strip of marzipan.

Brush the top of the cake with more melted jam, and fit on the marzipan lid. Trim the edges, and pinch together. Roll to give a smooth surface

Allow to dry uncovered for two days before applying the Royal icing.

For the Royal icing:

5 egg whites
2½ lbs (1.25 kg) icing sugar
2½ teaspoons glycerine
8 teaspoons lemon juice

To make the Royal icing:

Whisk the egg whites until slightly frothy.

Gradually add the icing sugar, beating well.

Add the glycerine and the lemon juice.

To ice and decorate the cake:

Pour the icing over the cake and smooth the top and sides with a palette knife.

Allow to harden for 24 hours before decorating with glacé cherries, citron shapes, and candle holders.

Put lighted candles into the holders just before serving.

Oven: 300°F/150°C Gas Mark 2

NORTH COUNTRY PIKELETS

Makes 6

Pikelet is the north country name for crumpets. They are delicious served hot and buttered at teatime, or for high tea with a poached egg on top.

12 oz (350 g) plain flour
1 teaspoon bicarbonate of soda
½ oz (15 g) fresh yeast
½ pint (300 ml/ 1¼ cups) lukewarm water
½ teaspoon salt
2 teaspoons cream of tartar
¼ pint (150 ml/ ⅔ cup) milk

Mix the flour, bicarbonate of soda, yeast and water in a large bowl. Blend until smooth.

Cover with a polythene bag and leave at room temperature for about 1 hour until frothy.

Stir in the salt, cream of tartar and the milk.

Mix well to make a pouring batter, adding more milk if required.

Cover and leave to stand for about 20 minutes.

Grease and heat thoroughly a griddle or heavy frying pan, and six crumpet rings or 3 inch (7.5 cm) metal cutters.

Pour the mixture into the rings to a depth of about ½ inch (1 cm).

Cook until the mixture sets, then remove the rings.

When the tops of the pikelets are covered in holes (after a total cooking time of about 5 minutes), turn them over to cook for a further 3 minutes until lightly brown on the other side.

Cool on a wire rack.

Toast the pikelets lightly on both sides before serving hot and buttered.

SINGIN' HINNIES

This is a traditional Northumberland favourite. It is a type of girdle cake, made from a currant scone mixture and usually served, whilst hot, cut in half and buttered. It is called Singin' Hinnie because it hisses when the butter and cream melt on the hot girdle. It is said that mothers when asked by their children if the scones were ready to eat would reply: 'No, it's just singin' hinnies'. Hinny (honey) is a term of affection for children.

8 oz (225 g) plain flour
1 teaspoon baking powder
½ teaspoon salt
2 oz (50 g) butter
2 oz (50 g) lard
2 oz (50 g) currants
Milk and single or sour cream to mix
A little sugar

Sieve the flour, baking powder and salt into a bowl, and mix together.

Cut the butter and lard into small pieces.

Rub the fat into the flour mixture until it resembles fine breadcrumbs.

Add the prepared currants.

Mix with enough milk and cream to make a soft dough.

Knead lightly.

Roll out the dough on a floured board into an 8 inch (20 cm) round.

Bake on both sides for a total of about 20 minutes on a hot girdle until golden brown.

Originally a pair of 'singin hinnie hands were used to turn the scone over.

Alternatively a baking sheet can be placed over the sieve, turn over both the sheet and the girdle, so that the scone sits on the plate.

It should then be possible to slide the hinnie back on to the girdle with the cooked side on top.

If preferred the scone may be cut into quarters for easier cooking.

A large greased frying pan may be substituted for the girdle.

Serve hot, spilt, spread with butter and sprinkled with sugar if liked.

DUKE OF NORTHUMBERLAND CAKE

From the receipt book of Margaret Crawhall dated 1854, obviously when days were more leisurely, since beating in the eggs alone took one hour and ten minutes.

1 lb (450 g) butter
1 lb (450 g) sugar
1 lb (450 g) flour
8 eggs
½ lb (225 g) currants

It is the beating which makes the difference.

Beat the butter to a cream.

Add the sugar and work it up for twenty minutes.

Add a well beaten egg one at a time and beat the mixture ten minutes between each addition.

Then add the flour gently and work for five minutes, and the fruit carefully last.

Bake in a moderate oven.

EASY BOILED FRUIT CAKE

Gentle cooking before baking causes the fruit to swell which makes this good value cake taste delicious.

12 oz (350 g) mixed fruit
4 oz (100 g) caster or brown sugar
4 oz (100 g) margarine or butter
¼ pint (150 ml/ ⅔ cup) water
1 egg
8 oz (225 g) self-raising flour

Place the fruit, sugar, fat and water in a saucepan.

Bring slowly to simmering point.

Cover the pan and simmer gently for 20 minutes.

Allow the mixture to cool.

Beat the egg thoroughly.

Stir into the mixture.

Sieve the flour.

Stir into the mixture to give a dropping consistency.

Put the mixture into a greased 6 inch (15 cm) cake tin.

Bake in a cool oven for 1½ hours.

Oven: 300°F/150°C Gas Mark 2

GEORDIE STOTTY CAKE

Stotty or stotty cyek (cake) is not a cake at all, but a round flat loaf — a complete meal in itself — when filled with cheese, cold meat and salad. Stotty was traditionally made from the last scrapes of dough on baking day. Also called oven-bottom bread it was baked at the bottom of the oven in the range, and was often eaten on the same day, whereas new loaves were considered to be indigestible until a day old. Stotty cakes were most popular among the north east mining folk, where they often formed part of the 'bait' for the miner to take down the pit.

1 oz (25 g) fresh yeast
A pinch of white pepper
½ teaspoon sugar
½ lbs (675 g) plain flour
½ teaspoon salt
Tepid water to mix

Crumble the yeast into a basin.

Add the pepper and sugar.

Mix to a paste with about 3 tablespoons of tepid water.

Put the yeast in a warm place for about 15 minutes until it becomes frothy.

Sieve the flour and salt into a basin.

Make a hole in the centre of the flour, and pour in the yeast.

Mix together to form a stiff dough. If required add a little more tepid water.

Knead the dough until all the flour is absorbed.

Cover the bowl with a cloth and leave to rise for approximately 1 hour or until doubled in size.

Roll the dough out on a floured board, and shape into 12 rounds about 2″ (5 cm) thick.

Put on a greased baking sheet and cook in a hot oven for about 25 minutes until golden brown.

Oven: 450°F/230°C Gas Mark 8

GRANDMOTHER'S TOFFEE

8 oz (225 g) sugar
1 tablespoon of water
1 tablespoon of golden syrup
1½ oz (40 g) butter
1½ teaspoons vinegar

Grease a 7 inch (18 cm) tin.

Put the sugar and water into a heavy-based saucepan.

Heat gently over a low heat until the sugar dissolves, stirring with a wooden spoon.

Add the remaining ingredients, and bring the mixture to the boil.

Boil rapidly without stirring until a little toffee dropped into a saucer of cold water hardens.

Remove from the heat.

Mark into squares just before setting point is reached.

PEPPERMINT CREAMS

A favourite recipe of Kenneth Gamblin the former verger of St. Michaels and St. Paul's, the Duke of Northumberland's church in Alnwick.

1 egg white
About 8 oz (225 g) icing sugar
Peppermint essence
Green food colouring

Place the egg white in a bowl and whisk until stiff.

Gradually mix in the sieved icing sugar with a wooden spoon to form a stiff paste, adding more icing sugar if required.

Mix in a few drops of peppermint essence and green food colouring, and knead well.

Roll the mixture into a long sausage shape on a board dusted with a little icing sugar.

Cut the roll into slices 6 inches (5 mm) thick.

Place on a sugared plate or tray and place in the refrigerator for about 1 hour to set.

CANDIED GOOSEBERRIES

An attractive tin of these sweetmeats makes an ideal gift.

1 lb (450 g) gooseberries
1 lb (450 g) granulated sugar
½ pint (300 ml/ 1¼ cups) water
Caster sugar for dusting

Choose sound, ripe fruit to be candied.

Wash and top and tail the selected gooseberries.

Put the sugar and water in a heavy saucepan.

Bring to the boil.

Boil, stirring to dissolve the sugar, until the mixture becomes a thick syrup, which will drop in beads from a spoon.

Drop in the berries.

Simmer for 10 minutes.

Leave the fruit in the pan, but set aside to become cold.

Boil the mixture up again and then pour on to a sieve to drain away the excess syrup.

Dip the gooseberries in caster sugar.

Arrange the fruit on a wire tray and put in a cool oven for 2-3 hours until dry.

Pack in a tin, putting greaseproof paper between the layers of fruit.

Oven: 275°F/140°C Gas Mark 1

MINCEMEAT

Mincemeat is used to fill mince pies, which are part of the traditional Christmas fare in Britain.

In medieval times meat was minced up and added to spices to help keep it fresh during the winter months. This is how the name of this preserve derived. Today meat is omitted from mincemeat, but the making of it survives from the Middle Ages.

8 oz (225 g) sultanas
8 oz (225 g) currants
8 oz (225 g) stoned raisins
8 oz (225 g) cooking apples
8 oz (225 g) chopped mixed peel
2 lemons
8 oz (225 g) dark brown sugar
4 oz (100 g) shredded suet
½ teaspoon ground nutmeg
½ teaspoon ground cinnamon
½ teaspoon of mixed spice
4 tablespoons rum or brandy (optional)

Wash, prepare the chop and dried fruit.

Peel, core and finely chop the apples.

Grate the rind and squeeze the juice from the lemon.

Add the sugar, suet, spices, lemon rind and juices and mix all together thoroughly.

Stir in the rum or brandy if used.

Cover the bowl, and leave the mincemeat to stand for 2 days.

Pack the mincemeat into jars, seal and store as for jam.

Keep for a few weeks before using.

Mincemeat keeps well and improves with storage.

For the best keeping properties use a firm cooking apple such as a Wellington.

THE MINISTER'S MARMALADE

Makes 5 lbs (2.25 kg)

This delicious mixed fruit marmalade has a fresh tangy taste.

1 large orange
1 lemon
1 grapefruit
2½ lb (1.25 kg) preserving sugar
1½ pints (900ml/ 3¾ cups) water

Grate the rind from the fruit.

Remove and discard any white pith.

Cut the fruit into small pieces.

Remove the pips.

Put the grated rind and cut up fruit into preserving pan with the sugar and water.

Boil the mixture for about 30 minutes until the rind is tender, and the marmalade is setting.

To test for setting point, spoon a little marmalade on to a cold saucer.

Push the marmalade gently with the little finger, and if it wrinkles it is set.

Stir well and pot.

Cover with purchased jam covers.

GREEN TOMATO PICKLE

A favourite recipe of Mrs Gamblin, wife of the former verger of St Michael and St Paul's, the Duke of Northumberland's church in Alnwick.

2 lbs (900 g) green tomatoes
½ cauliflower
1½ lbs (675 g) onions
2 oz (50 g) salt
2½ pints (6¼ cups) vinegar
2½ lbs (1.25 kg) brown sugar
5 oz (150 g) plain flour
2 teaspoons turmeric
2 teaspoons dry mustard
½ teaspoon grated nutmeg
½ teaspoon ground cloves
½ teaspoon ground ginger

Peel and chop the tomatoes.

Break the cauliflower into florets.

Peel and chop the onions.

Arrange the vegetables in layers in a bowl, sprinkling each layer with salt.

Cover with water and allow to stand overnight.

Drain and rinse the vegetables under running water.

Put 2 pints of vinegar and the sugar into a large heavy saucepan and bring to the boil.

Stir in the vegetables and bring to the boil again.

Mix all the remaining ingredients with the remaining vinegar and add to the pan.

Bring to the boil and simmer for 10 minutes or until the pickle is thick.

Pot and cover.

Best stored for 3 months before using.

RHUBARB CHUTNEY

4 lbs (1.75 kg) rhubarb
4 onions
1 lb (450 g) stoned dates
1 lb (450 g) demerara sugar
8 oz (225 g) sultanas
2 oz (50 g) salt
½ oz (15 g) chillies
A little cayenne pepper
1½ pints (900ml/ 3¾ cups) vinegar

Wash the rhubarb and cut each stalk into small pieces.

Peel and chop the onions.

Put the rhubarb, onions, dates, sugar, sultanas, salt, chillies, cayenne pepper and vinegar into a preserving pan.

Bring to the boil.

Then simmer, stirring frequently until the mixture is tender.

Allow to cool, pour into dry, clean jars, and cover with purchased jam covers, then with a round cloth, brushed with melted candle grease to make an air-tight seal.

APPLE CHUTNEY

6 lbs (2.75 kg) apples
2 lbs (900 kg) pickling onions
3 lbs (1.5 kg) brown sugar
2 pints (1.15 litres/ 5 cups) malt vinegar
1½ lbs (675 g) sultanas
2 oz (50 g) mustard seeds
2 teaspoons salt
½ teaspoon cayenne pepper

Peel, core and chop the apples.

Peel and chop the onions.

Put all ingredients into a large heavy saucepan.

Bring to the boil and simmer gently for about 1½ hours or until the chutney sets, and beomes thick.

Pot and seal.

MUSTARD SAUCE

Depending on the accompaniment this sauce can be made using milk mixed with half fish or chicken stock.

1 oz (25 g) butter or margarine
1 oz (25 g) plain or self-raising flour
½ pint (300 ml/ 1¼ cups) milk
1½-2 teaspoons dry mustard powder (according to taste)
½ teaspoon caster sugar
½ teaspoon vinegar
A little lemon juice
2 fl oz (3 tablespoons/ ¼ cup) double cream (optional)
Salt and pepper

Melt the butter in saucepan and stir in the flour.

Gradually add the milk stirring.

Bring to the boil, then simmer until the sauce thickens.

Blend the mustard powder, sugar, vinegar and lemon juice to a smooth cream.

Stir into the sauce.

Just before serving stir in the cream and season the sauce to taste with salt and pepper.

Heat through without boiling.

Serve with fried or grilled herring, mackerel or boiled chicken.

OLD CURRANT SAUCE FOR VENISON FROM RABY CASTLE

8 fl oz (250 ml/1 cup) port or ruby wine
2 oz (50 g) currants
½ teaspoon of powdered cloves
2 small slices of white bread, grated
2 oz (50 g) butter

Soak the currants in the wine for one hour.

Put the mixture into a saucepan with the cloves, and the breadcrumbs.

Add the butter and simmer gently for about 20 minutes until the bread softens and the mixture thickens.

This sauce freezes well, and can be made in larger quantities.

As well as venison, Old Currant Sauce is also good served with lamb or duck.

LEMON SAUCE   Serves 4

This sauce is traditionally served with Newcastle Pudding, but it is also delicious with plain steamed puddings.

4 oz (100 g) lemon marmalade
1 lemon

Grate the lemon rind and squeeze the juice.

Melt the lemon marmalade in a saucepan.

Stir in the lemon juice and rind.

Serve the sauce hot.

GOOSEBERRY KETCHUP

Young gooseberries make an excellent ketchup, which is delicious with cold meat.

4 lbs (1.75 kg) gooseberries
3 lbs (1.4 kg) demerara sugar
1 pint (600 ml/ 2½ cups) white wine vinegar
2 teaspoons of cloves
2 teaspoons of allspice
2 teaspoons of ground cinnamon

Wash, top and tail the gooseberries.

Put the fruit in a preserving pan with the sugar, vinegar and the spices.

Bring to the boil, and simmer slowly for 2 hours.

When cooked, allow to cool.

Put the ketchup into wide mouthed bottles and seal.

RHUBARB WINE

5 lbs (2.25 kg) rhubarb
1 gallon (4.5 litres) cold water
To every gallon of juice yielded from the above add:
    4 lbs (1.75 kg) sugar
    The juice and rind of 2 lemons
    1 oz (25 g) ginger (optional)

Cut the rhubarb into pieces and crush with a rolling pin.

Put into a stone jar or plastic bucket.

Add the water and cover the container.

Let it stand for 7 days.

Strain off the liquid and to every gallon of juice add 4 lbs (1.75 kg) sugar, the juice and rind of 2 lemons and, if liked, the ginger.

Let stand for 7 days longer, stirring every day.

Bottle and keep for one year before using.

FRUIT COOLER   Makes 3 pints (1.75 litres/ 6 cups)

1 pint (600 ml/ 2½ cups) pineapple juice
1 pint (600 ml/ 2½ cups) orange juice
1 pint (600 ml/ 2½ cups) bitter lemon
Ice
1 orange

Mix together thoroughly.

Add the ice before serving.

Garnish with slices of orange.

Acknowledgements:

Grateful thanks are extended to the many people of Northumbria who have contributed towards this collection of recipes especially:

Mrs. E. Hunter of Bedlington for Ginger Sponge Pudding, Eggs in a Bed, Fruit Cooler, Patty Toppers, Prize Winning Baked Herrings, Ginger Sponge Parkin, John Peel Tart, Grandmother's Toffee, The Minister's Marmalade and Bible Cake, many of which came from her mother's recipe book dating from the late 19th century.

Mrs. A. Vaggs of Morpeth from Cottage Teatime Cake, Dark Gingerbread, Sweet Rose Pastry and Easy Boiled Fruit Cake.

Ralph Holmes & Sons (Fish Merchants) Ltd. of Berwick-upon-Tweed for Berwick-Style Salmon.

Mr. S. Brewer, City Librarian and Arts Officer, Newcastle-upon-Tyne City Libraries for Duke of Northumberland Cake from the receipt book of Margaret Crawhall 1854.

Bill Weeks, Lecturer in Agriculture and Food Marketing, University of Newcastle-upon-Tyne and Peggy Howie for Pigeon Pie with Brown Ale and Casserole of Kielder Venison in Lindisfarne Mead.

Van den Bergs and Jurgens Ltd. (Krona Spread), and Bill Weeks for Sarah's Pie (with kind permission of Sarah's son, Bill), and Leek and Goose Egg Flan.

Miss M. Dover of Newcastle-upon-Tyne for information and her niece Mrs. Gamlin for Green Tomato Pickle and Apple Chutney; and Kenneth Gamlin for Peppermint Creams.

Matthew Nicklin, Head Chef at Langley Castle Hotel, near Hexham, Northumberland for Lakins Elizabethan Delight and Citrus Fruit Chicken.

Micheal L. Hackett of Lindisfarne Ltd., Holy Island for information about Lindisfarne Mead.

John and Iben Broust-Cocker, Riverdale Hall Hotel, Bellingham, Northumberland for Pheasant in Lindisfarne Mead.

Kathy Williams of Sevenoaks, Kent for Bacon Broth and Old Nan's Panacklety from her Co. Durham grandmother's recipe book.

Margaret Morris of Consett, Co. Durham for Leek Pudding (with Bacon or Mince).

Jim Skeggs of Somerset for Trout in Cream.

Mrs. Edwards of Gateshead, Tyne & Wear for Granny's Pot Pie.

Martin O'Shea of Darlington, Co. Durham for the quotation and information.

THE COUNTRY RECIPE SERIES

Available now @ £1.95 each

Cambridgeshire
Cornwall
Cumberland & Westmorland
Derbyshire
Devon
Dorset
Gloucestershire
Hampshire
Kent
Lancashire
Leicestershire
Norfolk
Northumberland & Durham
Oxfordshire
Somerset
Suffolk
Sussex
Warwickshire
Wiltshire
Yorkshire

All these books are available at your local bookshop or newsagent, or can be ordered direct from the publisher. Just tick the titles you require and fill in the form below. Prices and availability subject to change without notice.

Ravette Books Limited, 3 Glenside Estate, Star Road, Partridge Green, Horsham, West Sussex RH13 8RA.

Please send a cheque or postal order, and allow the following for postage and packing. UK 25p for one book and 10p for each additional book ordered.

Name...

Address...

....

....